First World War
and Army of Occupation
War Diary
France, Belgium and Germany

62 DIVISION
Headquarters, Branches and Services
Commander Royal Engineers
2 January 1917 - 31 August 1919

WO95/3074/1

The Naval & Military Press Ltd
www.nmarchive.com
Published in association with The National Archives

Published by

The Naval & Military Press Ltd

Unit 10 Ridgewood Industrial Park,

Uckfield, East Sussex,

TN22 5QE England

Tel: +44 (0) 1825 749494

www.naval-military-press.com

www.nmarchive.com

This diary has been reprinted in facsimile from the original. Any imperfections are inevitably reproduced and the quality may fall short of modern type and cartographic standards.

© **Crown Copyright**
Images reproduced by permission of The National Archives, London, England, 2015.

Contents

Document type	Place/Title	Date From	Date To
Heading	WO95/3074/2		
Heading	62nd Division D.A. Dir. Ordnance Services 1917 Jan-1919 Aug		
War Diary	Redford Calais	02/01/1917	03/01/1917
War Diary	Ercheu-Le-Grand	04/01/1917	24/01/1917
War Diary	Bus-Les-Artois	26/01/1917	04/03/1917
War Diary	Engelbelmer	05/03/1917	24/03/1917
War Diary	Meraucourt	25/03/1917	05/04/1917
War Diary	Achiet Le Grand	06/03/1917	17/06/1917
War Diary	Achiet-le-Petit	18/06/1917	30/06/1917
War Diary	Monument Commomoratif	01/07/1917	31/07/1917
Heading	War Diary of D.A.D.O.S. 62nd Division From 1st August To 31st August 1917 (Volume 8)		
War Diary	Monument Commomoratif	01/08/1917	28/08/1917
Heading	War Diary of Capt R.M. Holland D.A.D.O.S. 62nd Division From Sept 1st 1917 To Sept 30th 1917 Vol 9		
War Diary	Monument Commomoratif	09/09/1917	30/09/1917
Heading	War Diary of Capt R.M. Holland D.A.D.O.S. 62nd Division From Oct 1st To Oct 31st 1917		
War Diary	Monument Commomoratif	01/10/1917	11/10/1917
War Diary	Haplincourt	12/10/1917	29/10/1917
War Diary	Fosseux	30/10/1917	31/10/1917
Heading	War Diary Vol XI Of D A D O S 62nd Division R M Holland November 1917		
War Diary	Fosseux	01/11/1917	14/11/1917
War Diary	Barastre	14/11/1917	23/11/1917
War Diary	Neuville	23/11/1917	28/11/1917
War Diary	Haplincourt	29/11/1917	30/11/1917
Heading	War Diary of Capt R.M. Holland D A D O S 62nd Division December 1917		
War Diary	Haplincourt	01/12/1917	04/12/1917
War Diary	Basseux	04/12/1917	05/12/1917
War Diary	St. Catherines	06/12/1917	10/12/1917
War Diary	Labeuvriere	11/12/1917	18/12/1917
War Diary	Meugouil	19/12/1917	31/12/1917
Heading	War Diary of Capt R.M. Holland D A D O S 62nd (West Riding) Division January 1918 Volume XIII		
War Diary	Mingoval	01/01/1918	07/01/1918
War Diary	Sh. Catherines	08/01/1918	31/01/1918
Heading	War Diary of Capt R.M. Holland D A D O S 62nd (West Riding) Division Volume XIV February 1918		
War Diary	St Catherine	01/02/1918	09/02/1918
War Diary	Tincques	10/02/1918	28/02/1918
Heading	War Diary of Deputy Assistant Director Of Ordnance Services 62nd Division From 1.3.18 To 31.3.18 Volume XV 1918		
War Diary	Tincques Ecuire	01/03/1918	23/03/1918
War Diary	Darlus	24/03/1918	25/03/1918
War Diary	Fonquevillers	26/03/1918	27/03/1918
War Diary	Souastre	28/03/1918	31/03/1918

Heading	War Diary of Deputy Assistant Director Of Ordnance Services 62nd Division From 1-4-18 To 30-4-18 Vol 16		
War Diary	Pas	01/04/1918	06/04/1918
War Diary	Henu	07/04/1918	16/04/1918
War Diary	Pas	17/04/1918	26/04/1918
War Diary	Authie	27/04/1918	30/04/1918
Heading	War Diary of Deputy Assistant Director Of Ordnance Services 62nd Division From 1-5-18 To 31-5-18 Volume 17 1918		
War Diary	Authie	01/05/1918	15/05/1918
War Diary	Pas	16/05/1918	31/05/1918
Heading	War Diary of Deputy Assistant Director Of Ordnance Services 62nd Divn From 1-6-18 To 30-6-18 Vol XVIII 1918		
War Diary	Pas	01/06/1918	30/06/1918
Heading	War Diary of Deputy Assistant Dir Of Ordnance Services 62nd Div From 1-7-18 To 31-7-18 Vol 19 1918		
War Diary	Pas	01/07/1918	17/07/1918
War Diary	Tours	17/07/1918	31/07/1918
Heading	War Diary of Major R.M. Holland D.A.D.O.S. 62nd (WR) Division August 1918		
War Diary	Bisseuil	01/08/1918	05/08/1918
War Diary	Pas	06/08/1918	31/08/1918
Heading	War Diary By Major R.M. Holland Deputy Assistant Director Of Ordnance Services 62nd (West Riding) Division Volume XXI 1918		
War Diary	Courcelles-le-Couple	01/09/1918	20/09/1918
War Diary	Gommecourt	22/09/1918	30/09/1918
Heading	War Diary of Major R.M. Holland D.A.D.O.S. 62nd (WR) Division Volume XXII October 1918		
War Diary	Gommecourt	01/10/1918	03/10/1918
War Diary	Royaulcourt	04/10/1918	06/10/1918
War Diary	Havrincourt	07/10/1918	10/10/1918
War Diary	Masnieres	11/10/1918	11/10/1918
War Diary	Estourmel	12/10/1918	31/10/1918
Heading	War Diary Major R.M. Holland D A D O F 62nd (West Riding) Division		
War Diary	Solesmes	01/11/1918	11/11/1918
War Diary	Souis-Le-Bois	12/11/1918	17/11/1918
War Diary	Ham-Sur-Haure	18/11/1918	20/11/1918
War Diary	Couillet	21/11/1918	24/11/1918
War Diary	Bioul	25/11/1918	26/11/1918
War Diary	Lecguoin	27/11/1918	30/11/1918
Heading	War Diary of Major R.M. Holland D.A.D.O.S. 62nd (W.R.) Division Volume 24 1918		
War Diary	Lecguoin	01/12/1918	10/12/1918
War Diary	Harnoir	11/12/1918	12/12/1918
War Diary	Vielsalm	13/12/1918	16/12/1918
War Diary	Malmedy	17/12/1918	20/12/1918
War Diary	Schleiden	21/12/1918	31/12/1918
Heading	War Diary of Major R.M. Holland R A O Corps D.A.D.O.S. 62nd (WR) Divn From 1st January 1919 To 24th January 1919 Volume I		
War Diary	Schleiden	01/01/1919	24/01/1919

Heading	War Diary of Major R.M. Holland D.A.D.O.S. 62nd (West Riding) Division Volume XXVI February 1919		
War Diary	Schleiden	01/02/1919	28/02/1919
Heading	War Diary of Major R.M. Holland D.A.D.O.S. Highland Division Volume III March 1919		
War Diary	Schleiden	01/03/1919	12/03/1919
War Diary	Duren	13/03/1919	31/03/1919
Heading	War Diary of Major R.M. Holland D.A.D.O.S. Highland Division Volume V May 1919		
War Diary	Duren	01/05/1919	31/05/1919
Heading	War Diary of Major R.M. Holland D.A.D.O.S. Highland Division Volume VI June 1919		
War Diary	Duren	01/06/1919	30/06/1919
Heading	War Diary of Major R.M. Holland D.A.D.O.S. Highland Division Volume VI July 1919		
War Diary	Duren Germany	01/07/1919	31/07/1919
Heading	Diary Of D.A.D.O.S. Highland Division Volume VIII August 1919		
War Diary	Duren Germany	01/08/1919	11/08/1919
War Diary	Clipstone	12/08/1919	31/08/1919

WO95/30741/2

62ND DIVISION

D.A.DIR.ORDNANCE SERVICES

~~JAN 1917-DEC 1918~~

1917 JAN — 1919 AUG

Army Form C. 2118.

WAR DIARY
or
INTELLIGENCE SUMMARY.
(Erase heading not required.)

Instructions regarding War Diaries and Intelligence Summaries are contained in F.S. Regs., Part II. and the Staff Manual respectively. Title pages will be prepared in manuscript.

DADS 628M
January 1917 Vol I

Place	Date	Hour	Summary of Events and Information	Remarks and references to Appendices
Bedford	2.1.17		Left Bedford for Overseas	
Calais	3.1.17		Arrived at Calais was instructed to report to D.A.D.S. was referred to H.Q. 3rd Army. Was unshunted temporary High. Car Division to Etaples - le Grand. Heavier Clothing for Div. had been returned and arranged	
Etaples - le Grand	4.1.17		to receive it and distribute to Units on their arrival	
	5.1.17	6.1.17	Clothing commenced to arrive and was handed issued unit on arrival	
	8.1.17	9.1.17		
	10.1.17	11.1.17	do	
	12.1.17			
	13.1.17	14.1.17	Divisional Headquarters arrived and my Staff arrived	
	15.1.17		Routine work	
	16.1.17		Went America re local purchase	
	17.1.17	18.1.17	Routine work	
	19.1.17		Went with D.A.Q.M.G. Behancourt respecting move of Division	
	20.1.17		Saw Aberathe re Ordnance Stores	
	22.1.17		Moved with Division to Bernaval	
	23.1.17		do	Lt. Burdee-Atkins
	24.1.17	25.1.17	Routine work	

Army Form C. 2118.

WAR DIARY
INTELLIGENCE SUMMARY.
(Erase heading not required.)

January 1917

Place	Date	Hour	Summary of Events and Information	Remarks and references to Appendices
Hq-Cov-	26-1-17		Visited V Army Headquarters & also Lieut. Col. Taylor - brought back Lieut. Morris	
Arbois	27-1-17		Rajlheap — routine work	
	28-1-17		Routine work	
	29-1-17		3 Armourers called in from units & Div. Armourers Shop.	
	30-1-17		Routine work	
	31-1-17		do.	

R M Anderson Capt
DADOS 62nd Division

WAR DIARY

INTELLIGENCE SUMMARY.

(Erase heading not required.)

Army Form C. 2118.

WADOS 6 2Army February 1917 Vol 2

Place	Date	Hour	Summary of Events and Information	Remarks and references to Appendices
Rue de Artois	1-2-17		Amiens re purchases	
	2-2-17		Commenced distribution of Box Respirators	
	3-2-17		Journeyed re Ordnance supplies with A.O.C.	
	4-2-17		Completed issue of Small Box respirators	
	5-2-17		Routine work. Gun Boots repairs undertaken by 2 A.O.C. from Corps Paris	
	6-2-17		Visited Amiens re Ordnance Services	
	7-2-17		Routine work	
	8-2-17		Arrival of 49 West Riding	
	9-2-17		Routine work	
	10-2-17		Completed 49 West Riding with heavy Clothing & special vehicle	
	11-2-17 12-2-17		Routine work	
	13-2-17		Lieut Col Stanifords left the Division and was replaced by Lieut Col McGaffin	
	14-2-17		Routine work	
	15-2-17		Amiens re purchases	
	16-2-17		Routine work	
	17-2-17		Shot trenchon Came into operation	

Army Form C. 2118.

WAR DIARY
or
INTELLIGENCE SUMMARY.
(Erase heading not required.)

Instructions regarding War Diaries and Intelligence Summaries are contained in F. S. Regs., Part II. and the Staff Manual respectively. Title pages will be prepared in manuscript.

Place	Date	Hour	Summary of Events and Information	Remarks and references to Appendices
Bus le Artois	18.2.17		Beauvais arranging unloading and storing of stores owing to lorries being stopped on account of thaw precautions	
	19.2.17		Beauvais re stores Doulens re - removal of Office & dump	
	20.2.17		Routine work	
	21.2.17		Luncheon in Amiens	
	22.2.17		Routine work	
	23.2.17		Saw A.D.V.S. re shoe supplies of stores from Base	
	24.1.17		Purchase 3000 Bags full Canvas	
	25.1.17		Railhead changes from Beauvais to Belle Eglise. Serving difficulties arising owing to lorries being stopped causing lack of Transport, and not being able to distribute stores in a proper manner.	
	26.1.17		As above but at Beauvais Railhead full of stores regulations changed, no place to stack stores at Belle Eglise. Ammunition horse transport and stores arrive at train trucks full of rubbish	
	27.1.17		Instructions received re convoy to Doncourt	
	28.1.17		Unloff received Cremant bedunne stores dent	

A M Arthurs Capt
SADVS 62nd Division

WAR DIARY

INTELLIGENCE SUMMARY

Army Form C. 2118.

SA 505
62nd Division
Vol 3

Place	Date	Hour	Summary of Events and Information	Remarks and references to Appendices
Bus les Artois Englebelmer	1917 Mar	1	Large quantities of stores arrived at Railhead owing to lorries not running due to frost precautions. Distribution as far as possible made from Railhead. The	
		2		
		3	Stores were dumped on the ground and issues made. All the lofts were at Railhead & work in consequence was disorganised.	
"		4	Moved stores to Forceville and office to Engelbelmer. Permission was granted to run lorries from Bus to Forceville, but there were more stores for mines than lorries could carry in one trip, in consequence some stores had to be left for collection at late date. Part of S.F. waggon was used for office furniture to Engelbelmer.	
Englebelmer		5	Forceville Fixing up of Ordnance dump to Div. Dump	
		6	Lorries down from Railhead	
		7	Railhead changed to Acheux. Obtained permission from lorries to Varennes to clear stores dumps but not all taken away by units. Ordnance line struck arrived Acheux.	
		8	Permission given for lorries to run Acheux.	
		9	Lorries could run to Forceville. Dumps at Forceville changed to Englebelmer. Lorries running for 36 hours.	

WAR DIARY or INTELLIGENCE SUMMARY

Army Form C. 2118. Sheet (2)

Place	Date	Hour	Summary of Events and Information	Remarks and references to Appendices
Englebelmer	Mar 10		Lorries again stopped and unable to clear from Beaucourt, Beau[court] & Grecville. Had to run staff to Acheux to slaughterhouse.	
		#13	Lorries allowed to run 2 hours in order to clear stores at various places	
		17/14 15 16	Issuing old ration stores	
		17	Made application to run lorries, again provided our difficulties is carrying on work owing to lack of transport	
		18	Ration changes to run lorries to Acheux	
		19	Railhead changes to Beauval, but unable to get lorries up on account of state of roads.	
		20	Lorries in consequence sent back to Acheux.	
		21	Receives instructions from ? to Miraumont	
		24	Unable to get lorries to Miraumont on no accommodation	
	25		Obtained empty patched huts near Railhead. Sent stores to Acheux by lorry	
Miraumont			thence to Miraumont by train, roads very bad.	
	26		Lorries came in pack train but for 2 lines only stopped any lorries in Miraumont to clear all trucks, and trains when back to Acheux partly loaded.	

Army Form C. 2118.

3rd Sheet

WAR DIARY
or
INTELLIGENCE SUMMARY.
(Erase heading not required.)

Instructions regarding War Diaries and Intelligence Summaries are contained in F.S. Regs., Part II. and the Staff Manual respectively. Title pages will be prepared in manuscript.

Place	Date	Hour	Summary of Events and Information	Remarks and references to Appendices
Mouumont	Mar 27		Train stayed in & therefore all trucks cleared.	
	30		Advance arriving during night. Overnight not running. Made special application to get up 2 car appliances from Engelbelmer.	
	31		Routine work.	

R M Allways Capt
DAPOS. 62nd Division

Army Form C. 2118.

WAR DIARY
or
INTELLIGENCE SUMMARY.
(Erase heading not required.)

T.A.D.T. 62nd Division   Vol 4

Instructions regarding War Diaries and Intelligence Summaries are contained in F. S. Regs., Part II. and the Staff Manual respectively. Title pages will be prepared in manuscript.

Place	Date	Hour	Summary of Events and Information	Remarks and references to Appendices
Miraumont	Apl	1	Permission was given to bring up lorries from Engelbelmer to Miraumont	
		2	to clear all stores left behind at Engelbelmer.	
		3	Instructions received to move to Achiet-le-Grand at an early date as	
		4	units being sent forward	
		5	Round routine work.	
Achiet-le-Grand		6	Moved to Achiet-le-Grand. Lorries forced up between Dumps in tents, no building being available. As lorries had to travel via Albert Bapaume the journey was equal to 70 miles instead of 53 miles of the direct road has been fit to	
		7		
		8		
		9		
		10		
		11	run lorries on. Stores were not stopped, as it was possible to issue all	
		12	stores to units	
		13		
		14		
		15		
		16	No outstanding feature.	
		17		
		18		
		19		
		20		
		21		
		22	All Gum Boots High returned to base	

Army Form C. 2118.

WAR DIARY
or
INTELLIGENCE SUMMARY.
(Erase heading not required.)

Instructions regarding War Diaries and Intelligence Summaries are contained in F. S. Regs., Part II. and the Staff Manual respectively. Title pages will be prepared in manuscript.

Place	Date	Hour	Summary of Events and Information	Remarks and references to Appendices
Achiet-le-Grand	Apl 23		Arrangements made for the return of Winter Clothing.	
	24			
	25			
	26		Routine work.	
	27			
	28			
	29			
	30			

R.M. Holland Capt
DADOS. 62nd Division

Army Form C. 2118.

WAR DIARY
or
INTELLIGENCE SUMMARY.
(Erase heading not required.)

DADOS
62nd Division

May 1914

Place	Date	Hour	Summary of Events and Information	Remarks and references to Appendices
Achiet le Grand	May 10th		Principally routine work. Supplies coming up well from Base.	
	May 11 to		Units requirements being met. Arrangements all complete for the return of Winter Clothing & supplies sent regularly to the various Dumps	
	May 16		to Army on Leave	
	May 23			
	May 26 to 30th		Winter Clothing continues to be returned. No outstanding features. Jim Curlews' Murlys for meat refer, and the "Sheepy" Days applicable to this time of the year supplies or indents for Meat devies in considerable arising of time this month with Salonika. Rhine provides transport whenever possible and sends very large consignments to railhead	

R.M.H. Large
Capt
DADOS. 62nd Division.

62

Army Form C. 2118.

DADOS.
62nd Division

Vol 6

WAR DIARY
or
INTELLIGENCE SUMMARY.
(Erase heading not required.)

Instructions regarding War Diaries and Intelligence Summaries are contained in F. S. Regs., Part II. and the Staff Manual respectively. Title pages will be prepared in manuscript.

Place	Date	Hour	Summary of Events and Information	Remarks and references to Appendices
Achiet le Grand	June 16th		Issue. Clothing & all sent down to various bases. Envelopes	
	June 17		of going convoys forward to re-equipping units of the coming out of the line. Newburg Lewis Gun parts however scarce.	
			No outstanding feature.	
Achiet le Petit	June 18		Headquarters moves from Achiet-le-Grand to Achiet-le-Petit and arrangements are made for the Ordnance to be transferred also.	
	June 19		Routine wk. W. instructing feature	
	June 20		Reorge from Achiet to the Monument [erased] commenced near Bapaume	
	21/22/23rd		Routine work	

R M Mellor
Capt.
DADOS 62nd Div.

Army Form C. 2118.

WAR DIARY
or
INTELLIGENCE SUMMARY.
(Erase heading not required.)

Army Troops 63rd Division

Place	Date	Hour	Summary of Events and Information	Remarks and references to Appendices
Monument	July 1 – July 31		Took stock of Infantry Stores coming forward generally speaking very well. Revolver, Bags tool & spare parts for Lewis Guns, Binoculars Compasses and Wagon parts still not coming up as fast as wanted.	
	July 16		Staff of Divnl. H.Q. increased by additional 3 Officers from Infantry Battalions.	
		24	Such increase of Armoury making I in all.	
		25	Took Adv. D.A.D.O.S. withdrawn from and despatched to Base to assist inspection of various units Stores despatched to us than inspection of Field Artillery to be found or administration Div. Sergt. Armoury short of Equipment which up today was due to Reg. many moves in consequence of which they had not received their stores.	

(Sgd) R. M. Mallaby
D.A.D.O.S. 63rd Division

Original

Confidential
War Diary
of
D.A.D.O.S. 62ⁿᵈ Division

From 1ˢᵗ August to 31ˢᵗ August 1917.

(Volume 8).

Army Form C. 2118.

WAR DIARY
or
INTELLIGENCE SUMMARY.
(Erase heading not required.)

D.A.D.O.S.
6 2nd Division

Instructions regarding War Diaries and Intelligence Summaries are contained in F.S. Regs., Part II. and the Staff Manual respectively. Title pages will be prepared in manuscript.

Place	Date	Hour	Summary of Events and Information	Remarks and references to Appendices
Bonnieres Commandt. 6	Aug 1 to 7		Usual routine work, Inspection of Battalion stores received work at the Dump	
	Aug 8		252nd Army Field Artillery Bde. transferred to 3rd Division	
	Aug 9 to 16		Commenced preparation for Brevet quarters. Usual routine work	
	Aug 16		Lewis Guns. Inspection of Armourers	
	Aug 16 1.20 pm		inspection of Army with Division. I accompanied on this inspection. Routine work — no outstanding feature.	
	Aug 28		Went on leave.	

R M Allwya Capt
D.A.D.O.S. 62nd Division

ORIGINAL.

WO1 9

Confidential

War Diary

of

Capt. R. M. Holland. D.A.D.O.S. 62nd Division

From Sept 1st 1914 to Sept 30th 1914

Vol. 9

Army Form C. 2118.

WAR DIARY
or
INTELLIGENCE SUMMARY.
(Erase heading not required.)

DADS 62nd Division

Instructions regarding War Diaries and Intelligence Summaries are contained in F.S. Regs., Part II. and the Staff Manual respectively. Title pages will be prepared in manuscript.

Place	Date	Hour	Summary of Events and Information	Remarks and references to Appendices
	1917			
Monchiet	Sep 9		Relieved 32nd Division Knights	
Commencing		10	Very quiet day out	
		11	Enemy shelled Berthen 1000x field near gully	
			after light. Division commences move. See reports	
			Relieving 57th Division	
		12	Quiet day	
		13	Quiet day	
			Orders of advance sent to Brens Inf on Left of Brigade	
			rep to Group to move up. Deployment initiated west of Gonnelieu	
		17		
		18	Dublin emplt. Occupying Nube Quarry	
		19		
		20		
		21	Lieut Col J Adml inspected Division in rear & Engineers of Inf Bgd	
			Headquarters of B Div, came back after 31st J inspected both lines & the	
			new 2nd to line on Bgde westward. Lieutenant-Colonel her	
		26	Quiet day. In outskirting feature	
		27		
		29	Lt Col Blackburne handed 66th to Major	
			R W Major Caps	

Vol 10

Confidential

War Diary

Capt. R. M. Holland D.A.D.O.S. 62nd Division

From Oct. 1st to Oct. 31st 1917

WAR DIARY
INTELLIGENCE SUMMARY.
(Erase heading not required.)

Army Form C. 2118.

Instructions regarding War Diaries and Intelligence Summaries are contained in F.S. Regs., Part II. and the Staff Manual respectively. Title pages will be prepared in manuscript.

Place	Date	Hour	Summary of Events and Information	Remarks and references to Appendices
Monumont	Oct 1st to Oct 11		No outstanding feature. Supplies normal. Received warning to proceed to Hoplincourt	RA RA
at Hoplincourt	Oct 12		Removed to Hoplincourt. Transferred from VI to IV Corps	RA
	13		Second draught received for Brit[ish] use, also Boots, Gaiters,	RA
	14		Sheepskin, gloves etc. Division came out of line. Busy with	RA
	15		re-fitting and inspections	RA
	16			RA
	17			RA
	19			RA
	20		Stores came up well. Therefore Mobilisation stores being made up	RA
	22		quickly.	RA
	23			RA
	24			RA
	25			RA
	26		Artillery of XLC, MQ. 109 Coy train transferred to 57th Division. Issues	RA
			stopped from Base in consequence of impending move.	
	27		Sent all stores on hand for Artillery units to 57th Division. Two B/Category	RA
			men arrived from Base to replace two A/Category men being transferred to Infantry.	
	28		Individuals received warning to Observe x x Lyn [arrived] 460 & 4910s	"RA
			Out Coy to IV Corps Troops. Hebetus new kit at Doreins	"RA

WAR DIARY
INTELLIGENCE SUMMARY
(Erase heading not required.)

Army Form C. 2118.

Place	Date	Hour	Summary of Events and Information	Remarks and references to Appendices
Hapleucourt	Oct 1	29	Cleared all unserviceable stores to Sides. Loaded up 1 truck of stores & equipment for new railhead, as they could not be carried on lorries. Wired Bases to return supplies to new railhead.	RA RA RA
Gouzie		30	Removed to Gouzeau commenced new camp	RA
		31	Made necessary arrangements & commenced issuing stores.	RA

R M Milliner
Capt
DADOS 62nd Division

Vol II

War Diary

Vol XI

of

S.A.A.C. 62nd Division

R M Holland Capt
November 1917.

Army Form C. 2118.

WAR DIARY
or
INTELLIGENCE SUMMARY.
(Erase heading not required.)

DADOS
62nd Division

Instructions regarding War Diaries and Intelligence Summaries are contained in F. S. Regs., Part II. and the Staff Manual respectively. Title pages will be prepared in manuscript.

Place	Date	Hour	Summary of Events and Information	Remarks and references to Appendices
Sossons	Nov 11		Usual daily work. All equipment except few items not available from Base supplies.	Ref
	Nov 11	12	Complete weighing and overhaul of guns rifles. Artillery O.R.C. not very happy fill with 372nd Division. All stores arriving for Rearvista sent by Lorry to 37th Div.	Ref
	Nov 12		Received instructions to load up at Baroche, leave all except urgent stores at Sossons, to take only 1 tent and some stores during darkness.	Ref
		13	Selected men sent on advance party.	Ref
		14	Remove to Baroche with all staff except few who were left at Sossons to guard stores who be left behind.	Ref
Baroche	14th to 22nd		Commences drawing receiving operating stores supplies up for operations. Large quantities sent from Base supplies through IV Corps.	Ref
Neuville	Nov 23		Move to Neuville in order to be nearer army. Very busy daily lying	Ref
	Nov 28		urgent stores.	Ref

T2134. Wt. W708—776. 500000. 4/15. Sir J. C. & S.

Army Form C. 2118.

WAR DIARY
or
INTELLIGENCE SUMMARY.
(Erase heading not required.)

Instructions regarding War Diaries and Intelligence Summaries are contained in F. S. Regs., Part II. and the Staff Manual respectively. Title pages will be prepared in manuscript.

Place	Date	Hour	Summary of Events and Information	Remarks and references to Appendices

Original

Confidential

VOLUME XII

War diary

of

Capt. R. M. Holland DSO. 62nd Division

December 1917.

Original

WAR DIARY
INTELLIGENCE SUMMARY
(Erase heading not required.)

Army Form C. 2118.

Sheet 1

of 23rd Division

Place	Date	Hour	Summary of Events and Information	Remarks and references to Appendices
Staplehurst	Dec	1	Instructions were received that there was only a skeleton supply [staff?] at the new place and we would have to make arrangements to feed troops by rail	—
		2	Troops &c. as being transported by rail were not necessary to take delivery of stores, buy quantities of [?] can stoves were supplied	—
		3		—
		4	Owing to the troops going into line again, the orders for arrival was cancelled. This would be necessary to move again in two days time as he would never be the more nowhere.	—
Lassen		5	We decided practically no orders came in Luck which arrived	—
		6	Railway was not unloaded but Lt. Commgs [?] (neither Genl of Canteens) took one train 56th Division. Both talk getting	—
St Othmer		7	trays unloaded received instructions that truck myng again in a few days and was not to be here. 56th Division as they were just going out. As the 56th Division were staying on, we will take over the premises	—
		8	But in our ghost had cleared out and we just pulled out	—
Lussen		10	Moved to Lussen and received from the ghost the necessary	—
		11	evidence to re-occupy. All indents been checked up as given us the	—

Original   Army Form C. 2118.
                    Sheet II

WAR DIARY
or
INTELLIGENCE SUMMARY.
(Erase heading not required.)

Instructions regarding War Diaries and Intelligence
Summaries are contained in F. S. Regs., Part II.
and the Staff Manual respectively. Title pages
will be prepared in manuscript.

Place	Date	Hour	Summary of Events and Information	Remarks and references to Appendices
Lbowvien	Dec	12	Base. Men on left Inplacement the Artillery unity very	RA
		13	transferred to 4th Division, then later transferred them	RA
		14	to 2nd & 3rd Divisions	RA
		15	But whole reg was moved to Chininien	RA
		16	Transferred Europeans to Bracq	RA
		17	Received reinforcements men to Mergoil	RA
		18	Received reinforcements men to Mergoil	RA
Mergoil		19	Large quantities of stores arriving at Suidhead but owing to rain	RA
		20	moving they could not be delivered on in consequence they had	RA
		21	to be transported from Suidheir to Mergoil	RA
		22	L. Drove his lorry from Kane to Algido Dec 19th	RA
		23	very tryup of more first convoy large amounts for stores	RA
		24	together.	RA
		25		
		26	Saw successions but explore but withdrawn in my lines	RA
		27	At times snow to deep Rgt terrain made Rgt through and	RA
		28	some units unable to get through for stores	RA
		29	Artillery firing again Dec 31st Lost 6 days hostilities not been	RA
		30		
		31		RA

T2134. Wt. W708—776. 500000. 4/15. Sir J.C. & S.

Original Sheet III Army Form C. 2118.

WAR DIARY
or
INTELLIGENCE SUMMARY.

(Erase heading not required.)

Instructions regarding War Diaries and Intelligence Summaries are contained in F. S. Regs., Part II. and the Staff Manual respectively. Title pages will be prepared in manuscript.

Place	Date	Hour	Summary of Events and Information	Remarks and references to Appendices
			all English stores from Division to which they were attached 2/2 it Bde say 2nd Division supplies them very well.	Od Pd
			R.H. Wood Capt GSO2 62nd Division	

Original

Confidential

War Diary
of
Capt. R. M. Holland – DADOS 62nd (West Riding) Division

January 1918

Volume XIII

WAR DIARY or INTELLIGENCE SUMMARY

Army Form C. 2118.
Sheet I

62nd Division

Original

Instructions regarding War Diaries and Intelligence Summaries are contained in F. S. Regs., Part II. and the Staff Manual respectively. Title pages will be prepared in manuscript.

Place	Date 1918	Hour	Summary of Events and Information	Remarks and references to Appendices
Mingoval	Jan 1		Re-equipping of artillery units commenced. Continues for rest day	RA
	2		Heavy demand on personal equipment and horse shoes. Otherwise not special	RA
	3		Units re-equip	RA
	4		Reserve re-org division had to move to the gathering bays & Also	RA
	5		Re-equipping. Brigt 62nd Div Artillery returned & went to line with	RA
	6		January 13th when Bg. went exchange guns with 56th Division as the	RA
			latter were to leave Arras up the line. Arrangements were to put 56th Division to	RA
	7		trench men & go slow in restoration divisions	RA
	8		Returned to the authority of Army precautions for rainmen	RA
Mt Herine	9		Light artillery being in the event of new precautions being taken force.	RA
	10		Thus precaution not in operation all left rail way being defended	RA
			Garrison	RA
	11		The Rig stores by light railway not adequate and organised was necessity to the	RA
	12		extent that regard had then been but much better keeping as indeed.	RA
	13			RA
	28		On last to Arche Brighton	RA

WAR DIARY
INTELLIGENCE SUMMARY

Army Form C. 2118.

Sheet II

Original

(Erase heading not required.)

Instructions regarding War Diaries and Intelligence Summaries are contained in F. S. Regs., Part II. and the Staff Manual respectively. Title pages will be prepared in manuscript.

Place	Date 1916	Hour	Summary of Events and Information	Remarks and references to Appendices
St Catherine	Aug 29		Re-organising of Infantry Brigades. Disbanding of 3 Battalions	Ack
	30		Arranging for all stores to be sent in and keeping records of	RA
	31		specialists in accordance with D.R.O. instructions	RA

R M Thare
GSO 62nd (2nd) Division

Original

Confidential

War Diary

of

Capt. R. M. Holland.

9.T.O.O.* 62nd (West Riding) Division

Volume XIV

February 1918

YR/14

Original

WAR DIARY
INTELLIGENCE SUMMARY
(Erase heading not required.)

Army Form C. 2118.

Sheet 1
9 A.C.C.S.
62nd (West Riding) Division

Instructions regarding War Diaries and Intelligence Summaries are contained in F.S. Regs., Part II. and the Staff Manual respectively. Title pages will be prepared in manuscript.

Place	Date	Hour	Summary of Events and Information	Remarks and references to Appendices
Shirebury	Feb 9	1	Stores from disbanded units being sent in. Cheques with equipment collected. Several specials of reliefs were fairly good.	Ref
			Wire order received from 50th Division that Q.D. No. 9 were coming to 62nd Division. But they did not arrive until Feb 12th.	Ref
	2-9		Usual analysis work	Ref
Ingoes	10		Stores required. 135th Siege Bty 498 Bn R.G.A. Siege from 56th Division.	Ref
	11		Usual routine	Ref
	12		Stores Bty arrived equipped as Heavy Bty. Also arrived & set every to be equipping K Surplus.	Ref
	13		Reorganisation of 9/63 Heavy & Med Motor Battery & arrangement with other Divisions. F.M.B. Trench Jones & XIII Corps Troops.	Ref
	14		Usual routine	Ref
	15/6			Ref
	17		153rd & 154th Bgds., with exception of R.B.A. Trench Jones, to XIII Corps Troops	Ref
	18		48th Bde. Heavy & B Battery arriving from XIII Corps Troops	Ref
	19		Medium Trench Mortar being re-organised. Z Battery ceased exist.	Ref

T2134. Wt. W708—776. 500000. 4/15. Sir J.C. & S.

Original

Army Form C. 2118.

Shut II
D. A. D. S.
62nd (W.R.) Div.

WAR DIARY
or
INTELLIGENCE—SUMMARY.
(Erase heading not required.)

Instructions regarding War Diaries and Intelligence
Summaries are contained in F. S. Regs., Part II.
and the Staff Manual respectively. Title pages
will be prepared in manuscript.

Place	Date	Hour	Summary of Events and Information	Remarks and references to Appendices
Troyes	1918 Feb 20		Usual routine	
	21		19th & 5th Bde transferred to XIII Corps Troops	P.A
	22		Arrived Feb 12. 6" Mortar being supplied to Machine Gun	P.A
	23		Usual routine	P.A
	24		Battalion received, but no instruction will received. All wishes	P.A
	25		Transport requires being found from Decoy Fort	P.A
	26			P.A
	27		Visited Ordnance Depot, Calais	P.A
	28		Arrangements made to remove to Cairn on Mar 1 & 2	P.A

R. M. Ayrst
Capt
D A D O S 62nd (West Riding) Division

T2134. Wt. W708—776. 500000. 4/15. Sir J. C. & S.

Original 27   Vol 15

Confidential
War Diary
of
Deputy Assistant Director of Ordnance Services, 62nd Division

From 1-3-18- to 31-3-18-

Volume XV 1918.

Original

Army Form C. 2118.

WAR DIARY
INTELLIGENCE SUMMARY.
(Erase heading not required.)

Instructions regarding War Diaries and Intelligence Summaries are contained in F.S. Regs., Part II. and the Staff Manual respectively. Title pages will be prepared in manuscript.

2nd (West) Division

Place	Date	Hour	Summary of Events and Information	Remarks and references to Appendices
Ecoivres	1918 Jan 1		Opening of month at Ecoivres	Cp
	2		Tour duty at Ecoivres	Cp
	3		Ammunition across Gouy-Servins	Cp
	14			Cp
	20			Cp
	21		Usual routine work. Instructions received re move to Mudlus	Cp
	22			Cp
	23			Cp
Mudlus	24		Moved Mudlus. Same day received instructions re move to Ayette	Cp
	25		Left Mudlus another year toques to Decquery. Orders given that it was to move to Ayette there however received instructions to move to Gouy-villages.	Cp
	26		Orders Engineers, the 6th year part showed which units	Cp
	27		Owing to billeting, moved to Souastre, showed to be supplies of engineers	Cp
Souastre	28		Moves in. All units going	Cp
	28		Orders received for Bar. 1 Brig. only might move at Headquarters	Cp
Souastre	29		Reconnaissance of Mudlus by covering parties of Coy. troops	Cp

WAR DIARY
INTELLIGENCE SUMMARY.

Army Form C. 2118.

Sheet I
G.H.Q.T.
62nd (2nd W.R.) Division

Place	Date	Hour	Summary of Events and Information	Remarks and references to Appendices
Nowshera	Nov 30		all urgent demands sent in	R/S
	31		Insp. of 4th Divisional Artillery	R/S
			No shoes were abandoned by men	R/S

R.M.M. Mayne
G.S.O.1 62nd (2nd W.R.) Division

Original

Confidential
War Diary
of
Deputy Assistant Director of Ordnance Services 62nd Division

from 1-4-18 to 30-4-18

Vol: # 16 1918

Army Form C. 2118.

GADD
62nd (2/L) Division

April 1918

WAR DIARY
or
INTELLIGENCE SUMMARY

(Erase heading not required.)

Original

Place	Date	Hour	Summary of Events and Information	Remarks and references to Appendices
S. Pas	Apl 1918	1	March Pas from Snoub in Division opening out of line.	Cy
		2	Received staff and stores which had been left at Volean	Cy
		3	we moved to Pad	Cy
		4		Cy
		5	As 4th Div. Arty. Amm Column Artillery was away from Hex Div. we had been supplying them with urgent needs. They have now been formally transferred to Ordnance services from 4th Div.	Cy
			In Ordnance services from 4th Div. Troops Dump of III Army Corps	Cy
		6	Began our last days re-equipping	Cy
		7	Front Hex on Division Dump into line	Cy
Hex		8		Cy
		9	Large supplies of stores coming up from Base to be equipped	Cy
		10	especially for 4th Div. Artillery who were dis-embarked about	Cy
		11	of stores owing to the nature of their operations.	Cy
		13		Cy
		14		Cy
		15		Cy
		16	March Pad thro Canvas Camp	Cy
Pad		17		Cy
		18	Routine work	Cy

WAR DIARY
or
INTELLIGENCE SUMMARY

Army Form C. 2118.

Place	Date	Hour	Summary of Events and Information	Remarks and references to Appendices
Authie	Apr 27	9.21 a.m. 30	Much Authie. Attacking artillery took shelter.	

Confidential
War Diary
of
Deputy Assistant Director of Ordnance Services 62nd Division

Vol 17
Original

From 1-5-18 to 31-5-18.

Volume $\frac{\text{V}}{17}$ 1918.

May 1918   WAR DIARY or INTELLIGENCE SUMMARY   Army Form C. 2118.

62nd (West Riding) Division

Place	Date	Hour	Summary of Events and Information	Remarks and references to Appendices
Authie	May 1		Return of [men] consigned to [Bude] Clothing to Base	
	2		All unimportant stores about this [period] [perhaps?] marked	
	3			
	4			
	5		Employed [mending] & [cleaning] with [return of] style [clothing]	
	6		to the 4th Divisional Artillery [are] therefore to [been] now	
	7		Division. They are well supplied with stores [attached] to them	
	8			
	9			
	10		Routine work. [No] outstanding feature	
	11			
	12			
	13			
	14			
	15			
Pas	16		Move to Pas. on Division going into the line. Division not engaged	
	17			
	18			
	19			
	20		Ordinary work. No special feature to report	
	21			
	22		[Sergeant] Reuss [from] Army School for [emphasis] on to	
	23		All [?] [clothing] [allowed] [return] to [Bude] [?] [?]	
	24			
	28			
	29		Nothing special	
	30			
	31		by General [?]	

T2134. Wt. W708—776. 500000. 4/15. Sir J. C. & 8.

WAR DIARY
or
INTELLIGENCE SUMMARY.
Army Form C. 2118.

Sheet I
G.S.O.I
62nd (West Riding) Division

Original

Place	Date	Hour	Summary of Events and Information	Remarks and references to Appendices
Pas	Aug 29		G.S.O.I visited an inspected dump	R.M
	30		" Inspecting Quartermasters stores	R.M
	31			R.M
				R.M Libraries
				G.S.O.I to 11th N Division

Confidential
War Diary
of
Deputy Assistant Director of Ordnance Services 62nd Divn.
from 1-6-18 to 30-6-18

Vol 18

Vol: XVIII / 1918

Army Form C. 2118.

9th Bn.
62nd (West Riding) Division

WAR DIARY
or
INTELLIGENCE SUMMARY.
(Erase heading not required.)

Original

Instructions regarding War Diaries and Intelligence Summaries are contained in F.S. Regs., Part II. and the Staff Manual respectively. Title pages will be prepared in manuscript.

Place	Date	Hour	Summary of Events and Information	Remarks and references to Appendices
9/18	Jan	1 pm	[illegible handwritten entry]	RA
	2		[illegible]	RA
	3		2/5 Divisional Artillery were transferred to the 42nd Division	RA
			[illegible] cases only 1 post of machine guns [illegible]	RA
			[illegible] during the [illegible]. They were made up	RA
			from 62nd Divisional Bgd.	RA
	4		[illegible] Battalions were left in our Division in place of	RA
			9th West Yorks and 9th West Ridings	RA
	5		[illegible] work	RA
	6		13th Devons and 9th Hants left our Division	RA
	7		The Battalion were up [illegible] on [illegible] on [illegible] day. They had to get reduced to	RA
	8		[illegible] and 9th [illegible] Regiment were to be met by the [illegible]	RA
	9		Roads in 9th/11th was much torn up	RA
	10		Lorries [illegible] carrying personnel from 9th West Yorks & 9th West Ridings	RA
	11		and a great number of necessary [illegible] were transferred to	RA
	13		the two incoming Battalions	RA

T2134. Wt. W708-776. 50000. 4/15. Sir J. C. & S.

Army Form C. 2118.

Sheet II

WAR DIARY
or
INTELLIGENCE SUMMARY.

(Erase heading not required.)

Original   62nd Division

Instructions regarding War Diaries and Intelligence Summaries are contained in F.S. Regs., Part II. and the Staff Manual respectively. Title pages will be prepared in manuscript.

Place	Date	Hour	Summary of Events and Information	Remarks and references to Appendices
Qu	Jan 1st	14	Orders that 94th Brig taken off Battle order.	QA
Qu		15	Reply from Brig to be in readiness ready for despatch	QA
		16	Ditto	QA
		17		QA
		18	Rec'd wire when being with Europe Battalion stores	QA
		19		QA
		20		QA
		21	57 I.A. transferred to 1st Queen's	QA
		22	Orders rec'd by 6.36 Lense from Battalion	QA
		23	69 Queen's Officers and 10 ranks re-engagement leave	QA
		24	Record Rendic with	QA
		25	— do —	QA
		26	— do —	QA
		27		QA
		28		QA
		29		QA
		30		QA

R.M.Whyte
B/Gen 62nd Division

Confidential   Vol 19

War Diary

of

Deputy Assistant Dir: of Ordnance Services "62nd Div."

From 1. 7-18   to 31. 7-18

Vol ~~19~~ 19. 1918

WAR DIARY

INTELLIGENCE SUMMARY.

(Erase heading not required.)

Army Form C. 2118.

D.A.D.S.
62nd Division

Place	Date 1918	Hour	Summary of Events and Information	Remarks and references to Appendices
Pas	July	1st	Divisional Staff set up at Pas. Equipment almost complete. Exception of Blankets for Devons & Medical gowns. Routine work.	Ref
		2nd	do No satisfactory feature.	Ref
		13	do	Ref
		14	Devons proceed by train to unknown destination. Buses went to get shoes.	Ref
		15	Entrained at Mondicourt. Two truck loads of shoes arrived with rifles and were attached to train.	Ref
		16	Arrived at Mailly. Attached to XXII Corps. Dumped stores at railhead. No lorries were not available for removal.	Ref
		17	Shelters in French Camp at Mailly and move office to Mairie along with Divisional head quarters. Army Day Tournament drawn up by Balance were played off high jumps, jumps, weights through & on Cup balance at Mailly. Superior Jean Barr still on open.	Ref
Mary		18	Owing to rumour of withdrawal of Division only few men for despatches. Buses delivered by lorries & sent up lines.	Ref
		19	— do —	Ref

Army Form C. 2118.

WAR DIARY
or
INTELLIGENCE SUMMARY.
(Erase heading not required.)

Original 62nd Division

Place	Date	Hour	Summary of Events and Information	Remarks and references to Appendices
Camp	Feby 20		Supplying of urgent shoes received in response to telegrams.	Rf
	21		Troops being dealt with in usual way.	Rf
	22		General equipment to be handed over to our troops.	Rf
	23			Rf
	24		Bulk of stores kept at Marseilles awaiting urgent stores enough up to forward area	Rf
	25			Rf
	26			Rf
	27			Rf
	28		Marched to Division went move out of area & gave Mis Barn to supply stores.	Rf
	29		Valuable stores that we are going	Rf
	30		back to IV Corps.	Rf
	31		In progress being made with labour.	Rf

R.W. Arthur Maj
DADOS 62nd Division

WR 20

Volume VII

War Diary

of

Major R. M. Holland
D.A.D.O.S. 62nd (WR) Division

August 1918

Sheet 2

Army Form C. 2118.

G.S.O.
62nd (West Riding) Division

WAR DIARY
of
INTELLIGENCE SUMMARY.
(Erase heading not required.)

Instructions regarding War Diaries and Intelligence Summaries are contained in F. S. Regs., Part II. and the Staff Manual respectively. Title pages will be prepared in manuscript.

Place	Date 1916	Hour	Summary of Events and Information	Remarks and references to Appendices
Disseuil	Aug	1st	Three-four-hour-four. Move to Disseuil Div'l retired all stores possible	RA
		2	Troops above being received as well as intelligence to our Tree	RA
		3	Troops lads up, except those at Railway sidings at Therouanne	RA
		4	Four valley that were at Railway trucks up at presence	RA
		5	Arrived at Pas. End train-loads nighted Therouanne	RA
Pas.		6	G.S.O. began training personnel of Div. Several trucks at Therouanne from Base	RA
		7	Commenced issuing stores urgently required such as tools, picks & saw-units Repr. ambulance, all Staffs etc to enquire numbers of guns, vehicles &c deficient	RA
		8		RA
		9	Unit supplying with equipping of Division being checked and stores & &c	RA
		10	D.o.G. visits from RE	RA
		11	Visiting units. Gun. Park etc	RA
		12	Attended Conference by Maj. OR P. at G.S.O. Conference	RA
		13		RA
		14	Such advice from Base with stores to be equipment	RA

Army Form C. 2118.

Sheet II

GASD
62nd (West Riding) Division

WAR DIARY
or
INTELLIGENCE SUMMARY.
(Erase heading not required.)

Place	Date	Hour	Summary of Events and Information	Remarks and references to Appendices
Pas	1917 Aug	15	Moved Quartre along old Division Headquarters	Rt
		16	Reorganisation & new arrivals withdrawn	Rt
		17	Considering made to units	Rt
		18	Usual routine work	Rt
		19	Instructions received to move to VI Corps area	Rt
		20		Rt
		3pm	On leave to U.K.	Rt

R. M. Mayer
Major
GSO1. 62nd Division

Instructions regarding War Diaries and Intelligence Summaries are contained in F. S. Regs., Part II. and the Staff Manual respectively. Title pages will be prepared in manuscript.

T2134. Wt. W708—776. 500000. 4/15. Sir J. C. & S.

19 WD 21

War Diary
by
Major. R. M. Holland
Deputy Assistant Director of Ordnance Services
62nd (West Riding) Division.

Volume $\overline{XXI}$ 1918.

Sheet I

Army Form C. 2118.

D.A.D.O.S. 62nd (West Riding) Division

WAR DIARY
or
INTELLIGENCE SUMMARY.
(Erase heading not required.)

Instructions regarding War Diaries and Intelligence Summaries are contained in F. S. Regs., Part II. and the Staff Manual respectively. Title pages will be prepared in manuscript.

Place	Date	Hour	Summary of Events and Information	Remarks and references to Appendices
Courcelles le Comte	6/3 1918	3	On tour to Hinges - Kingdom	RA
		4	Returned from tour. Division out of line & re-equipping & refitting.	RA
		5	Officer at Courcelles and dump at Bienvillers. Arranged for refit & re-equipment	RA
			Armourer, Saddler & Boot repairing to come under Corps at Courcelles	RA
		7	Re-equipping as fast as possible. Such arriving at Achiet-le-Grand	RA
		8	every morning about midday by rail afternoon. Lee Crew torries to Achiet le Grand railhead.	RA
		9/9	Artillery re-joined from 38th Division.	RA
		10	Division moving up to line.	RA
		11	Lot of guns furnished by Artillery showed 5 guns left in O.M.W.O. dump	RA
			destroyed.	RA
		12		RA
		13	As Division is in action stores being delivered to wagon lines & dump.	RA
		14		RA
		15	Visited Sydney dumps	RA
		16	Special trip to United Kingdom	RA
		20	Returned from tour. Dump & refit removed to Sommecourt.	RA

T2134. Wt. W708—776. 50000. 4/15. Sir J. C. & S.

WAR DIARY
or
INTELLIGENCE SUMMARY.

(Erase heading not required.)

Army Form C. 2118.

Sheet II
9800 62nd (2nd R) Division

Instructions regarding War Diaries and Intelligence Summaries are contained in F. S. Regs., Part II. and the Staff Manual respectively. Title pages will be prepared in manuscript.

Place	Date	Hour	Summary of Events and Information	Remarks and references to Appendices
Connecourt	Sep. 22		Orders 12,000 Blankets & 1200 ground sheets issued	R A
	23		Routine work	R A
	24		Instructions received as to Division moving up line again	R A
	25		Leaving special articles for battle such as sandbags etc.	R A
	26		Divisional Headquarters moved to Beauval, but Ordnance Dump remained	R A
	27		Great supply Blankets by lorries arrived	R A
	28		Visited Headquarters at Beauval	R A
	29		Visited Headquarters at Beauval. Arranged move dump to an earlier date	R A
	30		Visited all Brigades in regard to supplies of stores	R A

T.J.134. Wt. W708—776. 50C000. 4/15. Sir J. C. & S.

NU 22

Volume XXII
October 1918
—
War Diary
Major R. M. Holland
D.A.D.O.S. 62nd (2nd R) Division

Army Form C. 2118.

9908
62nd (West Riding) Division

WAR DIARY
or
INTELLIGENCE SUMMARY.
(Erase heading not required.)

Instructions regarding War Diaries and Intelligence Summaries are contained in F. S. Regs., Part II. and the Staff Manual respectively. Title pages will be prepared in manuscript.

Place	Date 1918	Hour	Summary of Events and Information	Remarks and references to Appendices
Sauvincourt	Oct	1	Large supplies of Winter clothing coming forward	R/
		2	Instructions not up as Division coming out of line not coming forward as announced	R/
		3	Selected a site between Royaulcourt and Hermies	R/
Royaulcourt		4	Moved to Royaulcourt, with also Velu	R/
		5	Brigade changed to Havrincourt	R/
		6	Received instructions to move to Havrincourt	R/
Havrincourt		7	Moved to Havrincourt	R/
		8	Re-fitting of Division	R/
		9	Lectures, sulhead changing to Marnières	R/
		10	Moved to Marnières same day Lectures and went to Esnes wood	R/
Marnières		11		
Esnes wood		12		R/
		13	G.O.C. units were unable to escape blackdriving & ordered moving covering	R/
			Taken to Esnes ready at Havrincourt	R/
		14	Routine work	R/
		15	Bullhead moved to Cambrai Annex	R/
		16	Routine work	R/
		17	Laws arriving late at railhead in consequence lorries being substituted	R/

T2134. Wt. W708—776. 50000. 4/15. Sir J. C. & S.

Army Form C. 2118.

SAOO1
62nd (2nd) Division
Sheet II

WAR DIARY
or
INTELLIGENCE SUMMARY.
(Erase heading not required.)

Instructions regarding War Diaries and Intelligence Summaries are contained in F. S. Regs., Part II. and the Staff Manual respectively. Title pages will be prepared in manuscript.

Place	Date 1918	Hour	Summary of Events and Information	Remarks and references to Appendices
Edouard	Oct 18		Divisional Headquarters moved to Béville	R.A.
	19		Advis railhead proving to Aurvingt	R.A.
	20		Searched suring day	R.A.
	21		Gueir Landing of railheads all day	R.A.
	22		Routine work	R.A.
	23			R.A.
	24		Visited units to dump that had been left in back area & arranged & removal	R.A.
	25		Defend store dump	R.A.
	26		Routine work	R.A.
	27			R.A.
	28		Units holding nice view of finding new dumps	R.A.
	29		Routine work	R.A.
	30		Searches & visits to places visits to place & forced to be removed	R.A.
	31		Division still in reserve during owing to breakdown on railway	R.A.

R. M. Luckett
Lt Col GSO1 62nd (2nd) Division

Vol. 23

War Diary

Volume XXIII

November 1918.

of

Major R. M. Holland.

G.S.O.1. 62nd (West Riding) Division

R M Holland
Major

D.K.O.?
62nd (2/R) Division Army Form C. 2118.

Original

WAR DIARY
INTELLIGENCE SUMMARY
(Erase heading not required.)

Sheet I

Place	Date	Hour	Summary of Events and Information	Remarks and references to Appendices
Solesmes	Nov	1	Re-equipping regiments with stores.	R.A.
		2	— do —	R.A.
		3	— do —	R.A.
		4	— do —	R.A.
		5	Division reinforcements & recruits were moving every day consequently very	R.A.
			were not taking delivery of stores	R.A.
		6	Stores coming up from Base and accumulating as Dumps in view of R. Consignes	R.A.
		7	Routine work	R.A.
		8		R.A.
		9		R.A.
		10		R.A.
		11	Instructions received to move to Louis-le-Bois as Div. HQrs moving to this place	R.A.
Louis-le-Bois		12	Moved to Louis-le-Bois but railway still at Solesmes	R.A.
		13	Division instructed that it would not proceed to Rhine and Siegburg and	R.A.
			unnecessary stores would be returned	R.A.
			Ordered second quick Blanket	R.A.
		14	Large Quantities of surplus stores being returned in by units, as much as 12 lorry loads daily	R.A.
		15	Also indents coming forward for re-equipment	R.A.
			4th R.F.A. Bde Lounges to 62nd Div. Unable to get all references stores	R.A.
			Further owing to late being too far away in consequence about 15 lorry	R.A.

Original

WAR DIARY or INTELLIGENCE SUMMARY.

Army Form C. 2118.

G.H.Q.T.
2nd (OR.) Division
Sheet II

(Erase heading not required.)

Instructions regarding War Diaries and Intelligence Summaries are contained in F. S. Regs., Part II. and the Staff Manual respectively. Title pages will be prepared in manuscript.

Place	Date	Hour	Summary of Events and Information	Remarks and references to Appendices
Ham sur Heure	Nov 1	18	Lorries back left. The drivers collected had a good left in charge. Govt. IV Lorries who's army with 3rd army for clean.	P.M
			Moved from G.Bois. A further 30 lorries arriving owing to being very light & satisfactory enough.	P.M
		19	The lorry head altogether 15 lorries away to enable the work to be done, in addition.	P.M
			In had Ordnance stores not being brought up by park owing to its being very	P.M
			great shortage of lorries.	P.M
		20	Lorries very short to lorry head under new supply.	P.M
		21	Moved to Couillet	P.M
Couillet		22	Lorry head moved to Givry. Lorries were sent here for stores but more has arrived and new lorries sent as far Avesnes for clothing which was urgently required.	P.M
		23	Lorries again sent from Givry to other up stores. Very ult though they grumbled deal for Ham.	P.M
		24	Total of 50 lorries can hardly difficulty in carrying stores.	P.M
		25	Moved to Givry. Received reports that 112 lorries under lens.	P.M
Givry		26	Instructions to commence march to Leffrinck on 27th.	P.M
Leffrin		27	March began. Army to take lorries up to Givry. Lorries sufficient behind.	P.M

T2134. Wt. W708—776. 500000. 4/15. Sir J. C. & S.

Army Form C. 2118.

G.S.O.
62nd Division Sheet III

WAR DIARY
or
INTELLIGENCE SUMMARY
(Erase heading not required.)

Place	Date	Hour	Summary of Events and Information	Remarks and references to Appendices
Lesquin	Nov	28	Sent 2 bags to Sun Carbleet above Railhead sent to be opened at Ascq. Sent train not pierced 7 pm	RA
		29	Railhead gives that train arrived at 11 pm, but did not carry any Ordnance stores.	RA RA RA
		30	Sent railhead Although Rwuilhers has been at Douai Thursday no stores have yet arrived.	RA RA

R.W. Murphy
D.A.D.O.S. 62nd Division

Original

Confidential

War Diary
of
Major R. M. Holland
———
D.A.D.O.S. 62nd (W.R.) Division

Volume # 24
1918

WAR DIARY
INTELLIGENCE SUMMARY.
(Erase heading not required.)

Army Form C. 2118.

Instructions regarding War Diaries and Intelligence Summaries are contained in F.S. Regs., Part II. and the Staff Manual respectively. Title pages will be prepared in manuscript.

Place	Date	Hour	Summary of Events and Information	Remarks and references to Appendices
Legion	Dec. 1		Several trucks of stores that went re-consigned by R.T.O. below weight (I count)	Ref
	2		Wrongly recigned from T.R. Corps asking where re being kept. Claims	Ref
	3		T.R. Corps replies Ry. Plus are the Base and there were to fetched & new ones been brethren, losses arising & Ry. were to send them new recigned.	Ref
			All trains being despatched by "Rents Cancelled"	Ref
	4		Enquiries made as to new Ry. passes to schedule A	Ref
	5		Orders recd to schedule Bus. B. Tune was new wed to T.R. Corps note.	Ref
			Rents & pass under schedule A	Ref
	6		Schedule B being forwarded under schedule A.	Ref
	7		Galvin row T. buyers were duly notified by layer of new schedules B	Ref
	8		Company of traders. Bases arranging to send schedules B between ourselves	Ref
	9		All trucks from Base received. Nothing more on rail.	Ref
	10		Enquiries to Evere & Rouen	Ref
	11		Laillard moves to Bond	Ref
Rouen	12		Ourg. Cordon leaves Cuvelle & Base Rouen & Aubigny, Laguard	Ref

WAR DIARY

Army Form C. 2118.

Original — Sheet II
62nd (West Riding) Division

INTELLIGENCE SUMMARY
(Erase heading not required.)

Place	Date	Hour	Summary of Events and Information	Remarks and references to Appendices
Veidelia	Dec	13	Mark Veidelia. No stores received from Lahti	Ret
		14	Called on 20% I Corps rendezvous his shop of stores. Began to Bea	Ret
		15	Still no stores arrived as every Ohio railway vehicles have been commandeered	Ret
		16	No Hay. No grain	Ret
		17	Move to Maludy. Saw Lt. Col. B's of Russian Lancer's (getting nervous)	Ret
Maludy		18	Adv^d requisitioning from the hands	Ret
		19	Army received 8 tons of rail	Ret
		20	Nothing arrives at Maidhead	Ret
		21	Move to Lollades. 3 truck loads of oats arrived	Ret
Lollades		22	Stores now coming up in large quantities	Ret
		23	Army with delivery lorries for outlying Brigades by lorry	Ret
		24	Units to arrange to fetch met.	Ret
		25	Sailed 22 miles away at Eustrachen. 9½-10 hrs by rail (one way)	Ret
		26	Butterwick at Lollades	Ret
		27	Visited 4 500 number of units	Ret
		28	Nearly every truck arriving at Lollades is arriving in bits to be other	Ret

Army Form C. 2118.

WAR DIARY
of
Original INTELLIGENCE SUMMARY.

G.S.O.I. 62nd (2nd West Riding) Division
Sheet VII

(Erase heading not required.)

Instructions regarding War Diaries and Intelligence
Summaries are contained in F. S. Regs., Part II.
and the Staff Manual respectively. Title pages
will be prepared in manuscript.

Place	Date	Hour	Summary of Events and Information	Remarks and references to Appendices
Schivelen	19		Pilfering still going on by stores in transit	P.1
	20		Patrols sent to Metternich	P.1
	21		Routine work	P.1

R. M. Luce Major
G.S.O.I. 62nd (West Riding) Division

WD 25

D.A.D.O.S.
No..........
Date..........
(West Riding) Division.

Confidential

War Diary

of

Major R.N. Holland. R.A.O. Corps.

D.A.D.O.S 62nd (W.R.) Divn.

From 1st January 1919 to 24th January 1919.

(Volume I.)

Army Form C. 2118.

G.A.B.S.
62nd (2nd Reading) Division
Part I

WAR DIARY
INTELLIGENCE SUMMARY.
(Erase heading not required.)

Instructions regarding War Diaries and Intelligence Summaries are contained in F. S. Regs., Part II. and the Staff Manual respectively. Title pages will be prepared in manuscript.

Place	Date	Hour	Summary of Events and Information	Remarks and references to Appendices
Chiseldon	Jany 1919	1	Drew "Blankets" - orders from Base	R1
		2	Such arrivals from Base in almost every case with broken seals and contents	R1
		3	has been tampered with.	R1
		4	Ordnance stores not coming up well from the Base, probably due to shortage of	R1
		5	transport	R1
		6	Lt Kings purchase stores experiences with less deals of powder & tracing, but	R1
		7	now tht Baths are being established, & spare suits is being added.	R1
		8	Great difficulties made by staff to the investigation procure the letters	R1
		9	produced, but can be to spare any as work has not decreased	R1
		10	Undercrothing urgently required. No orders in return to our reserves.	R1
		11	Tax Training entered to wants	R1
		12	— for —	R1
		13	Such services as are being held in field. Few digs of having been lanterns with	R1
		14	interno congregations. Troops frequenting Sailbox	R1
		15	Routine work	R1
		16	Faith Everbrook Regarding Sailbox	R1

Army Form C. 2118.

Sheet I

DA&QMG
62nd (West Riding) Division

WAR DIARY
or
INTELLIGENCE SUMMARY.
(Erase heading not required.)

Instructions regarding War Diaries and Intelligence Summaries are contained in F.S. Regs., Part II. and the Staff Manual respectively. Title pages will be prepared in manuscript.

Place	Date	Hour	Summary of Events and Information	Remarks and references to Appendices
Scheven 1919	Jan	17	Reports attached staff seems very busy	RS
		18	Troops getting short supplies to B.O. clothing and being met in full	RS
		19	Uncle Hugh's orders become not of received. Serious	RS
		20	"Paides" Cologne. Requisition Ludermans etc	RS
		21	Routine work	RS
		22	"Paides" to the headquarters & other Corps Troops	RM
		23	Learn further news to date in regard to demobilising	RS
		24	Enquiry to learn when to ?	RS

R.M Morgan
Major
DAQMG 62nd (WR)
Division

T2134. Wt. W708—776. 500000. 4/15. Sir J.C.&S.

W 26

War Diary
of
Major R. M. Holland
D.A.D.O.S
62nd (West Riding) Division

Volume XXVI

February 1919

Original

WAR DIARY
INTELLIGENCE SUMMARY
(Erase heading not required.)

Army Form C. 2118.

9.7.05
62nd (West Riding) Division

Instructions regarding War Diaries and Intelligence Summaries are contained in F.S. Regs., Part II. and the Staff Manual respectively. Title pages will be prepared in manuscript.

Place	Date	Hour	Summary of Events and Information	Remarks and references to Appendices
Salisbury	Feby 11. 1914		On leave to United Kingdom	R.A.
	12		Examined the boys grievances and most coming up. Dissatisfaction of riding grenades	R.A.
	13		Drilling and Bomb especially life of 1/7 the letter also short	R.A.
	14		Child housing for Butts sweeping ground for recover ammunition etc	R.A.
	15		All men knuckle under of the Brigades convey exbvery well	R.A.
	16		Examined the re-organization of Army on the Continent to show	R.A.
	17		Standard accused of re-organization. Instructions received by GOC Batteries	R.A.
			a Conference	R.A.
	18		Attended Conference. Went was decided that definite steps could be taken for	R.A.
			our full nor particulars of relief Inspection arm to arrive	R.A.
	19		Out at Mill being received at my head with details broken shoes delivered	R.A.
	20		Duplicate issues being made to Base	R.A.
	21		Arrangements agreed that 63rd Division was not being broken up but eventually	R.A.
	22		Battalions being to be effected. The news changing to "Highland Division".	R.A.
	23		Visited tail head at Mechwigel	R.A.
	24		Dodd B. to take in place of GC 73rd Division arriving	R.A.

Original

Army Form C. 2118.

A.D.O.S.
62nd (West Riding) Division
Sheet II

WAR DIARY
or
INTELLIGENCE SUMMARY.
(Erase heading not required.)

Place	Date	Hour	Summary of Events and Information	Remarks and references to Appendices
Lebede	Feb	25	O.C. 6th Durham Light Infantry handed over to 3rd Queens	A
		26	New 250 Base Drums received	A
			Nothing definite decided as to New Battalions schedules or Regular Bn Age Strength	A
		27	Supplies from Base just yet sufficient to enable Stock to be made up	A
			Rations lightly supplied, as per furnishing account	A
		28	Still nothing done for truck or Base. In search of Offices	A
			Supplies, vehicles when possible running from Base daily	A

Lebede 28.2.19

C.M. Moye
Major
A.D.O.S. 62nd (W.R.) Division

CONFIDENTIAL.

ORIGINAL.

War Diary
of
Major. R. M. Holland   D.A.D.O.S.
Highland Division
March. 1919

Volume III

Sheet 1

WAR DIARY
INTELLIGENCE SUMMARY
(Erase heading not required.)

Army Form C. 2118.

Instructions regarding War Diaries and Intelligence Summaries are contained in F.S. Regs., Part II. and the Staff Manual respectively. Title pages will be prepared in manuscript.

Orgn: Highland Division

Place	Date	Hour	Summary of Events and Information	Remarks and references to Appendices
Schleiden 10/9	Mar 1st		Supplies & transport coming up from Basseveld. Only a shortage in cooks & stoves	R.A.
	2		Pt. York Lorries transferred to 6. of Division	R.A.
			Pilferage from trucks to be decrease	R.A.
	3		Ft. Blackley (Royal Engineers) arriving from 9th Division	R.A.
	4		Rested Rifle Coys. Engineers at Endricher	R.A.
	5		Resuming work to sub-section work	R.A.
	6		— do —	R.A.
	7		— do —	R.A.
	8		— do —	R.A.
	9		1st Argyl. Regt. Higher arrived from 23rd Division. Ab. ⅘ Act	R.A.
	10		Instructions received for General Headquarters over known to Queen	R.A.
	11		Arrangements sent: a week to have orders by Regt. to Queen	R.A.
	12		Gates Queen arr. arrange Horses Officers etc.	R.A.
	13		Moves of staff over to Queen	R.A.
Queen	14		Owing to floods returned Recher not arranged. Hdrs is transferred to Queen	R.A.
	15		Trucks arriving from Base inform Division - moves Highland Division	R.A.

Army Form C. 2118.

WAR DIARY
of
INTELLIGENCE SUMMARY
(Erase heading not required.)

9th H.Q. Highland Division

Place	Date	Hour	Summary of Events and Information	Remarks and references to Appendices
Ouren	Mar	16	1st Highland units arriving from Ouren. Belgium as coming up the equipment and badly clothed.	O.R.
		17	In information being had of your hyph	O.R.
		18	They are going to be disbanded and reinforcements kwh is would be necessary.	O.R.
		19	bn-equip	O.R.
		20	All the 62nd Division Infantry units will be being disposed of to the Division	O.R.
		21	of during terror and being replaced by Infantry Battalions	O.R.
		22	Complaints being received in regard to some conflict of fuel uniforms.	O.R.
		23	with some by Bn. Unit commanders asking thereby new ones should	O.R.
		24	be supplied.	O.R.
		25	Morning Flay No 14th R.H.A. Bde is preparing an relate and being	O.R.
			replaced by 19th Array Bde	
		26	62nd Division transfers 114th or March not behind arrangement.	O.R.
		27	Division leagues on Jyndoff will be being on Mar	O.R.
		28	57 Loden Highlander arrives from England. Equipment for new being transferred	O.R.
			from 1st Bone Regt	O.R.
		29	Official. Hospital left R. Base not yet arrived. Look up with R.A.D	O.R.

Army Form C. 2118.

G.H.Q. Highland Division
Sheet 11

WAR DIARY
INTELLIGENCE SUMMARY.
(Erase heading not required.)

Instructions regarding War Diaries and Intelligence Summaries are contained in F. S. Regs., Part II. and the Staff Manual respectively. Title pages will be prepared in manuscript.

Place	Date	Hour	Summary of Events and Information	Remarks and references to Appendices
Cologne 1919	Mar 30 31		Trinity Sunday. Church parade Morning Left H.Q. near Redwitz to Cairo	R.A 2.A

Cologne
March & April 1919

R.M. Hastings
G.S.O.2 Highland Division

War Diary
of
R. M. Holland
Major. DADOS. Highland Division.

May 1919.

Volume V

Sheet I

Army Form C. 2118.

D.A.D.O.S. Highland Division

Instructions regarding War Diaries and Intelligence Summaries are contained in F. S. Regs., Part II. and the Staff Manual respectively. Title pages will be prepared in manuscript.

WAR DIARY
or
~~INTELLIGENCE~~ SUMMARY.
(*Erase heading not required.*)

Place	Date	Hour	Summary of Events and Information	Remarks and references to Appendices
DUREN	May		Stores are coming regularly from the Base, the indents are met promptly and stores reaching here in about 12 days time from date of indent. The pilfering from the trucks has practically ceased. Complaints are still being received from unit commanders in regard to the part worn kilts which are being issued. Some of these are in a good condition whilst others are very poor owing to their having not been turned and in other cases to bad repairing. Large quantities of articles are being supplied which were not supplied during hostilities. Special authorities are being given either to obtain supplies from the Base or to requisition and the latter is now assuming considerable proportions. I have on requisition and in course of issue hundreds of tables, buckets etc and thousands of Mugs & Plates. The correspondence in connection with all these matters has grown enormously and the bulk of one's time is devoted to office work. The Staff are pressing to be demobilized and there are indications that their release will take place within the next month or so. They are going to be replaced by compulsory transferred men, I understand, from the R.G.A	RA

T2134. Wt. W708–776. 500000. 4/15. Sir J. C. & S.

Army Form C. 2118.

WAR DIARY
or
INTELLIGENCE SUMMARY.
(Erase heading not required.)

Instructions regarding War Diaries and Intelligence Summaries are contained in F. S. Regs., Part II. and the Staff Manual respectively. Title pages will be prepared in manuscript.

51st Div.
Highland Division

Place	Date	Hour	Summary of Events and Information	Remarks and references to Appendices
DUREN	Aug 17		Army change-over takes place and Divisional HQ moves to 6th Cheshires Regt appointed	
	18		Army small movements. Interior economy	
	19		Unit in cars gives a great deal of pleasure to everybody	
	20		Instructions have been received that 16th Battalion is proceed with	
	21		destroyed and the 51st Battalion they have been taken	
	22			
	23		33rd Division been interchanged to Light Division	
	24		Instructions received for forming Regt Appx when leaving the	
	25		the 1st and 2nd troops. Both is undergoing the review of the	
	26		the 1st & 4th RHA Regts Hd Qrs 307 Battn and it 1st RHAC which	
	27		were checking in orders and equipment to return to England	
	28		received instructions that Hd Qr would hand all the equipment to	
	29		General meeting of Hd Qrs of town. IV Corps & the key	
	30		of leaving also. Has been arranged for all those who will be	
	31		handed in here	
			the equipment of the 51st Highland Division will be with England	

OC 51st Hd Qrs
Maj General
51st Bn Highland Division

T 4134. Wt. W708-776. 50000. 4/15. Sir J. C. & S.

Confidential.

War Diary
of
Major R. M. HOLLAND.
D.A.D.O.S.
Highland Division

Volume VI

June 1919.

Queen 24/6/19

Sheet 1

WAR DIARY
or
INTELLIGENCE SUMMARY.
(Erase heading not required.)

Army Form C. 2118.

9th H.L.I.
Highland Division

Instructions regarding War Diaries and Intelligence Summaries are contained in F.S. Regs., Part II. and the Staff Manual respectively. Title pages will be prepared in manuscript.

Place	Date	Hour	Summary of Events and Information	Remarks and references to Appendices
Bedford 1915	June	1	Stores are coming up very well from the Base, with the exception of one or two moving up battalions. No recruits are giving return a satisfactory manner.	RA
		2	There has been a check taking up the units and owing to many changes of Commanders many deficiencies have been discovered. Details have been	RA
		3		RA
		4		RA
		5	submitted to complete establishment.	RA
		6	Lt. Col. J. McGilvray being despatched this month 1st Lt. R. engages the	RA
		7	7th Gds Ambulance whose equipment is being specially sent to Corps.	RA
		8	Intelligence used in noting on them transport. You cannot know	RA
		9	being deducted are handling their stores with it is Corps C.S.	RA
		10	transhipment are I hope going warming but the Division may be taken up on	RA
		11	I arrive forward at short notice. Units have been instructed where we can	RA
		12	at a moor they can haveto dump Stores; they are unable to carry.	RA
		13	By a date to be specified when men first ordered up to Oligzag Camp	RA
		14	Lewis & Vickers guns shall aw to be drawn from Oligzag dept.	RA
		15	Orders received that an advance of men will be ordered at Oligzag when	RA
		16	Sir H. Laurie Brigadier has already commenced to move forward.	RA

WAR DIARY
INTELLIGENCE SUMMARY

(Erase heading not required.)

Army Form C. 2118.

Sheet I

G.H.Q.
Highland Division

Place	Date	Hour	Summary of Events and Information	Remarks and references to Appendices
Ourem	June 17		Visited Ourem and Leiria dumps	Ch
	18		Reconnaissance received ask more of Brig. Artillery	Ref
	19		More of Artillery are S.P.A. dept: power and to further notice	Ch
	20		Opened up HQrs at Ourem. Brit. Artillery still in Ourem, the stores as	Ch
	21		Ourem are still being kept open	Ch
	22		Found verbally that as "Peace" was likely (shortly?) it was improbable	Ch
	23		that any more troops forward would take place	Ref
	24		Forgues sends very probably return	Ref
	25		To whole of the staff eight in demobilisation hour left with two	Ref
	26		exceptions and it is expected they will have all departed during this year	Ref
	27		10 days. R.G.A. have been attacked to take the place of R.F.A. dumbkeys	Ref
	28		Visited Ourem to see the advanced dumps	Ch
	29		Instructions received that units returning from Ourem district	Ch
	30		Commenced the several stations from advanced dumps at Ourem	Ref

Capt. M. Kay
G.S.O., Highland Division

War Diary
Major R. M. Holland.
D.A.D.O.S. Highland Division

July. 1919.

Volume VI

Army Form C. 2118.

WAR DIARY
of
INTELLIGENCE SUMMARY.
(Erase heading not required.)

Instructions regarding War Diaries and Intelligence Summaries are contained in F. S. Regs., Part II. and the Staff Manual respectively. Title pages will be prepared in manuscript.

J.A.G.9 [?]
Zeppelin Division

Place	Date	Hour	Summary of Events and Information	Remarks and references to Appendices
Dover 1919	July 1st		Requisitioning conveyance, stores in Dover	Ap
Europe	2		Departed on 9 days leave to UK	Ap
	3rd-24th		Sent UK	Ap
	25		Resumed duty on completion of leave	Ap
	26		Enquiring investigating what occurred during absence	Ap
	27		— do —	Ap
	28		Interviewing recent[?] [?] present Office during ..... [?]	Ap
			and crew to carry on	Ap
	29		Proceeded to Hospital, on the 13th of June	Ap
	30		Routine work	Ap
	31		Forted Brigade etc	Ap

R.M.A.[?]
Major
[?] Zeppelin Division

DIARY of D.A.D.O.S. HIGHLAND DIVISION

Volume VIII

August — 1919

Clipstone
17.9.19

R.M. ?????
D.A.D.O.S. Highland Div.

WAR DIARY

INTELLIGENCE SUMMARY

Army Form C. 2118.

DADOS Sheet I
Highland Division

Place	Date	Hour	Summary of Events and Information	Remarks and references to Appendices
Dover	1919 Aug	1	Instructions received that the Division is to proceed to England. Units	R.J.
Germany		2	to be with their arms & equipment, weapons and no stores of [any] nature.	R.J.
		3	All Mobilization equipment except M.T. to be left behind in	R.J.
		4	Ordnance. Second Reserve MT to be taken by those units in Division that	R.J.
		5	require it, when Orders they are to hand over to Ordnance.	R.J.
		6	Detailed instructions issued to units in regard of returning stores,	R.J.
		7	large quantities of which coming in, but the Cologne Depot unable to cope	R.J.
		8	in consequence of [want] of stores clerks, also packing cases, packing materials etc	R.J.
		9	As DADOS moving to England today times necessary to keep few AB Clerks	R.J.
		10	moving to England	R.J.
		11	Arrived at Calais and embarked for Folkestone	R.J.
Clipstone		12	Arrived Clipstone Camp at 4.45 am	R.J.
		13	Setting up office in Camp	R.J.
		14	Re instructions re demob of [men] & re-equipment	R.J.
		15	obtaining particulars of present equipment	R.J.
		16	2nd Bn Seaforth arrive Clipstone, 1/5 Bn Gordons and 3rd Bn Cameron Highrs	R.J.

WAR DIARY
OF
INTELLIGENCE SUMMARY.
(Erase heading not required.)

Army Form C. 2118.

Place	Date	Hour	Summary of Events and Information	Remarks and references to Appendices
Alipore	Aug	17	Divisional Artillery spent & further commenced at Tufasberry	A
		18		A
		19		A
		20		A
		21		A
		22		A
		23		A
		24		A
		25		A
		26		A
		27		A
		28		A
		29		A
		30		A
		31		A

www.ingramcontent.com/pod-product-compliance
Lightning Source LLC
Chambersburg PA
CBHW081441160426
43193CB00013B/2346